Advanced

Discipleship

WILLIAM C. NEECE

Faithful for Over 60 Years of Ministry

Advanced Discipleship By William Neece
© 2007 William C. Neece

Reformation Publishers
242 University Drive
Prestonsburg, KY 41653
1-800-765-2464
rpublisher@aol.com

ISBN: 978-1-60416-920-1
Typeset by Myra Summers
Cover design by Mike Belcher

Printed in the United States of America

ADVANCED DISCIPLESHIP

Back to the Basics in Christian Living—Book 2

Lesson 1 – Christian Humility

Memory Verse: Romans 12:3

1. Define "humility." (Use dictionary if desired.)

2. What words in our Memory Verse speak of "humility?"

3. Of what three things does the Bible say we should NOT be "proud?" *(Jer. 9:23)*

4. In what can we "glory?" *(Jer. 9:24, Gal. 6:14)*

5. Does this mean we can be proud because we are saved and others are not? Explain. *(Eph. 2:8-9)*

6. List those things that result from "pride", as seen in the following Scriptures:

  a. *Psalm 10:2*

  b. *Proverbs 11:2*

  c. *Proverbs 16:18*

  d. *Proverbs 28:25*

7. List the results of true "humility," as seen in these Scriptures:

    a. *Psalm 10:17*

    b. *Psalm 25:9*

    c. *Proverbs 11:2*

    d. *Proverbs 22:4*

    e. *Matthew 18:4*

f. *1 Peter 5:5-6*

8. What three things does God require of a Christian? *(Micah 6:8)*

9. List persons from Scripture who showed "humility" in their attitude, and give the circumstances in each case:

   a. *Genesis 32:10*

b. *1 Samuel 9:21*

c. *2 Samuel 7:18*

d. *1 Kings 3:7*

e. *Matthew 3:14*

f. *Matthew 8:8*

g. *1 Timothy 1:15*

10. List persons from Scripture who showed "pride" in their attitude, and give the circumstances in each case:

a. *Exodus 5:2*

b. *2 Kings 5:11*

c. *2 Chronicles 32:25*

d. *Esther 3:5*

e. Daniel 4:30

11. When we are able to do something worthwhile, who should receive the credit? *(John 15:5)*

12. Tell what happened to Herod when he accepted honors that belonged to God. *(Acts 12:21-23)*

13. Who in Scripture is the best example of "humility?" *(Phil. 2:8)*

14. Tell a story from Scripture that demonstrates the "humility" of Jesus. *(John 13:3-17)*

15. How should the spirit of "humility" manifest itself in Christian leaders? *(1 Peter 5:3)*

16. What should a Christian never do? *(Jer. 45:5)*

17. What should a Christian always do? *(1 Peter 5:6)*

18. Why is this the best course to follow? *(Matthew 23:12)*

19. Summarize in your own words what the Bible teaches concerning "humility."

Lesson 2: Christian Subjection

Memory Verse: 1 Peter 5:5

1. Define "subjection." (Use dictionary if desired)

2. From the following Scriptures list the FOUR POWERS to which God has made us "subject":

    a. *Romans 6:13, James 4:7*

    b. *Ephesians 6:1-3, Colossians 3:20*

    c. *1 Thessalonians 5:12-13, Hebrews 13:7*

d. *Romans 13:1-7, 1 Peter 2:13-15*

3. Why is it needful that children be "subject" to their parents? *(Eph. 6:1-4, 4:14)*

4. List the responsibilities parents have toward their children:

    a. *Deuteronomy 6:7*

    b. *Proverbs 22:6*

    c. *2 Corinthians 12:14*

d. *Ephesians 6:4*

e. *1 Timothy 3:4*

f. *Titus 2:4*

5. Does either parent in a family have authority over the other? (*Gen. 3:16, Eph. 5:21-23, Col. 3:18*)

6. What is the meaning of the statement: "Submitting yourselves one to another in the fear of God" *(Eph. 5:21)*? How does this idea of MUTUAL SUBMISSION apply in family relationships?

7. In view of the Scripture passages we have considered, WHY should a Christian man or woman be especially careful in choosing a marriage partner?

8. What solemn responsibilities does the husband have toward the wife? *(Eph. 5:21-23, 1 Tim. 5:8)*

9. Why is it necessary that authority be given to certain persons in the church? *(1 Cor. 14:40)*

10. From where does this authority come? *(1 Cor. 12:28)*

11. What responsibility goes with this authority? (*James 3:1*– Compare other versions such as NIV or NASB)

12. From the following Scriptures give the names of persons who used their authority as church officers, and briefly state in each case the circumstances involved:

    a. *Acts 5:1-11*

    b. *Acts 8:18-22*

    c. *Acts 10:44-48*

    d. *Acts 13:1-3*

    e. *Acts 13:9-12*

f. *Acts 14:23*

g. *Acts 15:13-19*

13. Why should Christians be "subject" to the laws of their land? Give at least 5 reasons from the following passages. *(Rom. 13:1-5, 1 Peter 2:13-15)*

    a.

    b.

    c.

d.

e.

14. What did each of the following men teach concerning obeying civil rulers?

   a. Moses *(Exodus 22:28)*

   b. Solomon *(Ecclesiastes 8:2, 10:20)*

c. Ezra *(Ezra 7:26)*

d. Jesus *(Matthew 23:1-3)*

e. Paul *(Acts 23:5)*

f. Peter *(1 Peter 2:17)*

15. If the laws of the land are in conflict with the laws of God, which should we obey? *(Acts 5:29)*

16. List as many men from the Bible as you can who disobeyed a ruler or his laws because they were in conflict

with God's commands. In each case give briefly the circumstances:

a. *Daniel 3:8-18*

b. *Daniel 6:4-10*

c. *Matthew 2:7-12*

d. *Acts 5:40-42*

17. From where do parents, the church, and the civil government get their authority? Identify each one:

a. Parents

b. The Church

c. Civil Government

18. A teacher has authority over his pupils. From which of these three God-given authorities does the authority of

    a. A Christian school teacher come?

    b. A Sunday School teacher come?

    c. A public school teacher come?

19. In a paragraph explain in your own words WHY disobedience of any kind is really disobedience to God. Use Scripture if possible.

Lesson 3: Christian Courtesy

Memory Verse: Ephesians 4:32

1. Are we commanded in Scripture to be "courteous?" If so, in what passage? (Use concordance if desired)

2. What is the "Golden Rule?" *(Matthew 7:12, Luke 6:31)*

3. In your own words explain why anyone who followed the "Golden Rule" would be "courteous."

4. Why should we be respectful and "courteous" to all people? *(Gen. 1:26-27)*

5. From the following Scriptures list the individuals who showed kindness, and in each case briefly give the circumstances:

a. *Genesis 50:18-21*

b. *Exodus 2:16-17*

c. *Ruth 2:15-16*

d. *2 Samuel 9*

e. *Luke 10:33-36*

f. *Acts 16:33-34*

g. *Acts 28:1-2*

6. What is the command of Christ? *(John 15:12)*

7. From the following Scriptures list the things Christians do in keeping this command. *(Matthew 5:22, 25, 39, 40, 41, 42, 44)*

8. How does God treat those who reject Him? *(Matthew 5:45)*

9. Why should we not take "revenge" against our enemies? *(Rom. 12:19)*

10. How does the Bible teach that we should treat strangers? *(Ex. 22:21, Deut. 10:19, Heb. 13:2)*

11. How does it say we should treat the poor? *(Deut. 15:7, Psa. 41:1, Prov. 19:17, Matt. 19:21, Gal. 2:10)*

12. What are the rewards of giving to the poor?

   a. *Psalm 41:1*

   b. *Proverbs 19:17*

c. *Matthew 19:21*

13. According to *Prov. 19:17* would it be possible to become poor by giving all you have to the poor?

14. How should we treat the weak? *(Acts 20:35, Rom. 15:1)*

15. How should we treat those in bonds (jail) and with other troubles? *(Heb. 13:3)*

16. How should we treat orphans and widows? *(James 1:27, Ex. 22:22, Deut. 26:12-13)*

17. How should we treat those we do not particularly like? *(Col. 3:12-14)*

18. In a paragraph summarize what the Scriptures teach regarding "kindness" and "courtesy."

Lesson 4: Christian Giving

Memory Verse: 2 Corinthians 9:6-7

1. What is a "tithe?" Define the word. (Use dictionary if desired)

2. To whom should our "tithes and offerings" really be given? *(Lev. 27:30, Mal. 3:8-10)*

3. What is the most important thing in "Christian Giving?"

4. What is our great EXAMPLE in giving? *(2 Cor. 8:9)* Please explain your answer.

5. What is the real purpose in "Christian Giving?" *(2 Cor. 8:13-14, 1 Cor. 9:14, Mal. 3:10)*

6. What is the "storehouse" mentioned in the Bible? *(Mal. 3:10)*

7. Through what agency were gifts made in the New Testament? *(2 Cor. 8:16-24—especially verse 19)*

8. What are some of the rewards of "Christian Giving?" *(Mal. 3:10, Prov. 3:9-10, 11:25, 22:9, Isa. 58:10, Luke 6:38, 2 Cor. 9:6, Phil. 4:17)*

9. Is God dependent upon our offerings? *(Psa. 50:10-12)*

10. Are we dependent upon God for our material things? *(Phil. 4:19, Psa. 24:1)*

11. From the following Scriptures list some examples in "Christian Giving," and give the circumstances in each case:

    a. *Exodus 35:22*

    b. *1 Chronicles 29:9*

    c. *Ezra 1:6*

    d. *Luke 21:1-4*

    e. *Acts 4:34-35*

    f. *Acts 11:29*

g. *Philippians 4:14-18*

12. State in your own words the LESSON the Lord taught regarding "The Widow's Mite." *(Luke 21:1-4)*

13. List persons from Scripture who refused to give, and tell the results:

   a. *Matthew 19:16-22*

   b. *Acts 5:1-11*

14. From the following Scriptures list the ways in which we should give:

   a. *Deuteronomy 16:17*

b. *Matthew 6:3*

c. *Matthew 10:8*

d. *Romans 12:8*

e. *1 Corinthians 16:2*

f. *2 Corinthians 9:7*

15. The reason many people do not give is because of "greed." From the following Scriptures list the results of "greed" for wealth:

   a. *Proverbs 15:27*

   b. *Ecclesiastes 5:10*

   c. *Jeremiah 17:11*

   d. *1 Timothy 6:10*

   e. *James 5:3*

16. List persons mentioned in Scripture that were "greedy for gain." Give circumstances and results.

    a. *Joshua 7:21*

    b. *2 Kings 5:20-27*

    c. *Matthew 26:15-16*

    d. *Acts 16:19*

    e. *Acts 24:26*

f. *2 Peter 2:15*

17. In your own words summarize what the Scriptures teach regarding "Christian Giving."

18. Assume that you are making $1,200 per month. Tell how much of it you would give to the Lord, and through what avenues.

Lesson 5: The Christian's Tongue

Memory Verse: James 1:26

1. What warnings are given in Scripture concerning the use of our "tongue?"

    a. *Psalm 34:13*

    b. *Proverbs 13:3*

    c. *Proverbs 21:23*

    d. *James 1:26*

e. *1 Peter 3:10*

2. When you judge a person's character, how much of your judgment comes from the content and manner of his speech?

3. Compare *James 3:2-8* with *Matthew 15:18-20*. Is it really the "tongue" that is unmanageable, or is the source of the trouble elsewhere? Explain.

4. List as many ways as you can that the human tongue is sometimes used in dishonoring God:

   a. *Proverbs 10:18*

b. *Proverbs 17:9*

c. *Ecclesiastes 5:3*

d. *Ephesians 4:31*

e. *1 Timothy 5:13*

f. *James 4:11*

g. *Colossians 3:8*

h. *Colossians 3:9*

i. *Matthew 5:34-37*

5. In *Proverbs 6:16-19* we have "seven" things that God hates. How many and which ones of them have to do with "speech?"

6. What is "slander?" (Use dictionary if desired)

7. List persons from Scripture who were guilty of "slander," and give the circumstances and results in each case:

    a. *Genesis 3:4-5*

    b. *Genesis 39:5-20*

    c. *2 Samuel 10:1-4*

    d. *Job 1:11*

    e. *Amos 7:10*

f. *Luke 23:1-2*

g. *Acts 17:5-9*

8. See if you can harmonize the apparent contradiction of *James 3:8* and *James 1:26*. (*Matt. 15:18-20* and *2 Cor. 5:17* may be of help to you.)

9. To what things are good words likened in the Bible?

a. *Colossians 4:6*

b. *Proverbs 16:24*

c. *Proverbs 25:11*

d. *Ecclesiastes 12:11*

10. List as many ways as you can that the "tongue" can be used to honor God. *(Isa. 50:4, Deut. 6:7, Psa. 145:11, Gal. 6:1, Rom. 12:7, Eph. 5:19)*

11. List the results of speaking in a godly way.

    a. *Colossians 4:6*

b. *Titus 2:8*

c. *Proverbs 16:24*

d. *Ecclesiastes 10:12*

e. *Luke 24:32*

12. What effect does Christ's voice have upon those who hear it?

    a. Strangers *(John 7:46)*

b. Enemies (John 18:6)

c. Friends (John 3:29)

d. Believers—"sheep" *(John 10:4)*

e. Sinners (Rev. 3:20)

13. Summarize in your own words what the Bible teaches concerning your responsibility in regard to your "tongue."

Lesson 6: The Christian's Mind

Memory Verse: Philippians 4:8

1. From the Memory Verse list the kind of things about which we are told to think.

2. Does God know what we think? *(Psa. 94:11, 1 Cor. 3:20)*

3. Where is a person's character really established? *(Prov. 23:7)*

4. What are the results of evil thoughts? *(James 1:14-15)*

5. From each of the following Bible stories show how the sequence of evil thoughts, evil deeds, and then death followed one another.

    a. *Genesis 3*

    b. *Joshua 7:20-26*

    c. *2 Kings 5:20-27*

    d. *Acts 5:1-11*

6. In *Romans 1:21-32* we see the final terrible results of rejecting God. What are the three ways of thinking that God gives such people up to? (See Verses 24, 26, 28)

   a.

   b.

   c.

7. What are the final terrible results in these people's lives? *(Rom. 1:32)*

8. Of the "seven" things that God hates, which one has to do with our thinking? *(Prov. 6:16-19)*

9. What great judgment did God bring on the earth because of people's evil thoughts? *(Gen. 6:5-7* with *Gen. 7:17)*

10. List the things we are commanded concerning the use of our "mind."

    a. *Philippians 2:5*

    b. *Romans 12:2*

c. *Romans 12:3*

d. *Luke 12:29*

e. *Romans 12:16*

f. *Philippians 2:3*

11. What do you think it means to be "carnally minded?" (*1 Cor. 3:3*)

12. Can one be "carnally minded" and please God? *(Rom. 8:5-7)*

13. What do you think it means to be "spiritually minded?" *(Rom. 8:6)*

14. What are the results of being "spiritually minded?" *(Rom. 8:6)*

15. List the things a "spiritually minded" man would consider in his mind:

   a. *Psalm 1:2*

b. *Deuteronomy 8:5*

c. *Deuteronomy 32:7*

d. *1 Samuel 12:24*

e. *Job 37:14*

f. *Psalm 8:3-4*

g. *Haggai 1:5-6*

h. *Matthew 6:28-29*

i. *Hebrews 12:3*

16. What is the difference between the thoughts of men and the thoughts of God? *(Isa. 55:8-9)*

17. Does Jesus judge people by their "actions" or by their "thoughts?" *(Matt. 5:21-22, 27-28, 2 Cor. 5:10)*

18. What promise does God make to His trusting children regarding their minds? *(Phil. 4:7)*

19. What prayer should we offer to God every day regarding our speaking and our thinking? *(Psa. 19:14—copy this verse on your paper below)*

Lesson 7: Christian Chastity

Memory Verse: 1 Corinthians 6:18

Read Proverbs 7

The following terms will be used in the Scriptures we study. Look them up in a dictionary so you will know their meaning:

"Adultery"

"Fornication"

"Lasciviousness"

"Harlot"

1. What does it mean to be "chaste?" (Use dictionary if desired)

2. We read, "Keep thyself pure" *(1 Tim. 5:22)*. What did our Lord say of those who are "pure in heart?" *(Matt. 5:8)*

3. What is a Christian's "manner of life" to be like? *(1 Peter 1:14-16—"conversation" means "manner of life")*

4. What is the source of evil desires? *(Mark 7:21-23)*

5. On what basis does God judge sins of impurity? *(Matt. 5:28)*

6. How do persons planning this type of sin usually deceive themselves? *(Job 24:15)*

7. In reading through *Proverbs 7*, list the five names and things the young man is likened to that show he is acting unwisely:

    a.

    b.

    c.

    d.

    e.

8. Who may be certain of God's judgment upon them? *(Heb. 13:4)*

9. With what should the tempted ones fill their minds? *(Psa. 119:9, John 17:17)*

10. To whom should they turn for help? *(Rom. 7:24-25)*

11. What should a Christian's attitude be toward sins of impurity? *(Eph. 5:3-7)*

12. What is *Ephesians 5:4* referring to? What does this practice show about a person's mind?

13. What command is given to Christians regarding persons known to be "fornicators?" *(1 Cor. 5:9)*

14. Why do you think such a command is necessary? *(Prov. 2:12-17)*

15. Against whom is the "fornicator" sinning? *(1 Cor. 6:18)*

16. What provisions has God given to protect us from this sin? *(Gal. 5:16, Psa. 119:11, 1 Cor. 7:2)*

17. List as many things as you can that Satan uses to try to ensnare us in sin.

18. In your own words summarize the importance of "chastity" in the life of a Christian.

Lesson 8: Christian Honesty

Memory Verse: 1 Thessalonians 4:11-12

1. What is the meaning of the word "honest?" (Use dictionary if desired)

2. How should Christians treat other people? *(Luke 6:32)*

3. Before whom should we provide things "honest?" *(2 Cor. 8:21)*

4. What are Christians to the unsaved world? *(2 Cor. 3:2-3)*

5. What kind of effect would "dishonesty" have on the above mentioned function?

6. What effect will a Christian's "honesty" have on unbelievers? *(1 Peter 2:12)*

7. What happens to those who practice "dishonesty?" *(Job 5:12-13)*

8. List all the deeds you can think of that would be listed under the heading of "dishonest":

   a. *Jeremiah 22:13*

b. *Leviticus 19:11*

c. *Proverbs 20:10*

d. *Leviticus 19:36*

e. The "10 Commandments" *(Exodus 20:1-17)*

f. Others:

9. What should we do if a Christian deals with us "dishonestly?" *(1 Cor. 6:7-8)*

10. Why should Christians never lie? *(Col. 3:9-10, Eph. 4:25)*

11. Who originated "lying?" *(John 8:44)*

12. In whom does the Lord delight? *(Prov. 12:22)*

13. What effect does "lying" and other such sins have on our prayers? *(Isa. 59:1-3)*

14. What does the popular saying, "Honesty is the best policy" mean?

15. On the basis of what we have learned about "honesty," is there anything wrong with the saying in question 14? Explain your answer.

16. Summarize in your own words what the Bible teaches about being "honest."

Lesson 9: Christian Faith

Memory Verse: Hebrews 11:6

1. What is the Bible definition of "faith?" *(Heb. 11:1)*

2. From where do we get "faith?" *(Eph. 2:8)*

3. What method or instrument does God use in giving this gift of "faith?" *(Rom. 10:17)*

4. What part does "faith" play in salvation? *(Eph. 2:8)* Explain your answer.

5. What is the result of refusing to "believe on the Lord Jesus Christ?" *(John 3:18)*

6. Why is "unbelief" such a terrible sin? (Think of whose Word is being doubted.)

7. What part does "faith" play in the living of our Christian lives? *(Rom. 1:16-17, Heb. 10:38)*

8. What was accounted unto Abraham as a result of his "faith?" *(Rom. 4:3)*

9. What is accounted to us as a result of our "faith?" *(Rom. 3:22)*

10. What part does "faith" play in our prayers? *(James 1:5-6)*

11. What part of a Christian's armor is called "faith?" *(Eph. 6:10-20*—especially notice Verse 16 and explain its significance)

12. From the following Scriptures and context, list persons who showed great "faith," and briefly give the circumstances:

    a. *Genesis 22:8*

b. *1 Samuel 17:37*

c. *Daniel 3:17*

d. *Acts 27:25*

13. From the following Scriptures and context, list persons
    who showed a lack of "faith," and briefly give the
    circumstances:

    a. *Numbers 11:21*

    b. *Matthew 17:19-20*

c. *Luke 1:20*

d. *Luke 24:11*

e. *John 20:25*

f. *Acts 12:14-15*

14. From *Hebrews 11:1-31* list 10 persons who acted upon "faith," and indicate what they did:

a.

b.

c.

d.

e.

f.

g.

h.

i.

j.

15. From your reading of *Hebrews 11*, would you say that our "faith" is judged more from what we SAY or what we DO?

16. The Scripture statement: "The just shall live by faith," led to the conversion of Martin Luther. List the four Scripture verses in which this quotation is found. (Use concordance if desired)

a.

b.

c.

d.

17. What prayer concerning "faith" should every Christian pray repeatedly? *(Luke 17:5)*

Lesson 10: Christian Worship

Memory Verse: John 4:23-24

1. What kind of people is God the Father seeking to "worship" Him? *(John 4:23)*

2. "Worship" includes the following five things. Tell what each of them means. (Use dictionary if desired)

   a. "Adoration"

   b. "Thanksgiving"

   c. "Petition"

d. "Intercession"

e. "Meditation"

3. Whom only are we to "worship?" *(Matt. 4:10)*

4. What did Peter say when Cornelius tried to "worship" him? *(Acts 10:25-26)*

5. What did the "angel" say when John tried to "worship" him? *(Rev. 22:8-9)*

---

6. What do you think is the difference between "admiring" a great man and "worshipping" God?

7. Make a list of people who "worshipped" Christ:

   a. *Matthew 2:11*

   b. *Matthew 8:2*

   c. *Matthew 9:18*

   d. *Matthew 14:33*

e. *Matthew 15:25*

f. *Matthew 28:9*

g. *Mark 5:6*

h. *Luke 24:52*

i. *John 9:38*

8. Did Jesus permit people to "worship" Him? Explain why.

9. Read *Isaiah 6*. When Isaiah really "saw the Lord," what did he find out about:

   a. The angel's ("seraphim's") opinion of the Lord.

   b. His own character.

   c. The character of other people he knew.

   d. His responsibility to carry out the Lord's wishes.

10. After studying *Isaiah 6*, do the following:

   a. List the human attitudes that cannot go along with true "worship."

   b. List the attitudes which are necessary for true "worship."

11. What will be our desire when we really get close to the Lord? *(Phil. 3:7-14)*

12. What attitude should we have when we enter a church building or other place of "worship?" *(Psa. 100:4)*

13. In *Psalm 107* compare Verses 8, 15, 21, and 31. What do you discover? Find other Psalms where we are repeatedly told to "praise" or "worship" the Lord.

14. Our Memory Verse says we should "worship" God "in Spirit and in truth." Write a paragraph telling what you think this means.